For Marsha and Christopher John

The Canadian Publishers
McClelland and Stewart Limited
25 Hollinger Road, Toronto 374

Earle
Birney
Prop.

Rag

&

Bone

Shop

McClelland and Stewart Limited   Toronto/Montreal

order of poems

Up was down   was up   enchanted   & still is
or else to look back so far is to escape all gravities

Undergrad inseparables 4 years before in Canada
long bony me   longer bonier Slim
trails joined again haphazard here
on what a camping ground!   the Pacific's only City
(LA? actors & football colleges)   San Francisco   SF
men of the world now   we never called it Frisco
Our tent a 20$ furnished shack complete with fleas
propped on a gusty ledge of hill   no no   *the* Hill
(nostalgia overcomes me)   *Telegraph*   in 1930
before rich ladies conquered it with phallic towers

Stone eyes of Julio's goat   the weird joy
that first morning in our wobbly hideout
(revolving now some 15,000 light-mornings under/over)
to see them glaring down from that primeval rockcave
old Julio from Sardinia had built into his cellar
Down was up & sidewise & every map Italian
I'd prised the one window open to smell Freedom
Bohemia   our secret Latin Quarter
but what filtered through the dockweed demonstration
occupying the sheeptrack we had for lane
was purest ramstink   It punched me stumbling
through all the 6-yard length of our new Home
to the back porch   a broomcloset on stilts
where Slim's long nose was sniffing too   grape mash
steaming straight up from someone's blissful lilybed

It's taken some forty years for me to know which smells
& frenzies last: the sound of laughter's with them
though only Slim knows if that's what he hears now
For me the happy waves surprise   fade in on any station
or else I'd give up tuning in at all
I have to think hard what my worries were

tremendous surely for us both at 25   bad as now
Slim freshly jilted & dropped from a newspaper back home
his novels   my poems   lost somewhere on that virgin moon
Slim selling pickles in SF   me Remedial English in UCal
(both mainly to non-buyers)   o yes I'd flunked the Phoo Dee
for thoughts about Eng. Lit. not in the lectures
In 2 months I'd be a jobless foreigner
Something had started the papers called Recession? Depression?
& me engaged to Susie   fellowslave & holdout for a wedding
Yes   & all that hasnt left me one good stink for savoring

It was Old Berkeley   true   the air still innocent
of crude oil oratory or tear gas   Beside uptight Philology
a clean brook ran through woods (long murdered)
& the few rebels walked   & Susie met me with a lunch
Sweet potato & eucalyptus   sick smells of academia
its boardinghouses & its sweatshops & fake scholars
Escape was on the Hill   Hell the bloody themes
could be marked in SF & ferried back to Berkeley (they were)
Meantime Susie   violet-eyed & fabulous   would wait of course

Lucky devils   it seemed we had it all   updown&sideways
or would have   once we achieved Sicilian mistresses
mastered Italian   made pals with the real citizens
those blackhanded stevedores from Naples   & Julio. . .
Somehow only the mothers handled English
Used it when they collected rent or laundry   Except Maria
of the Lilies   who decided we were friends not Feds
& sold us something even she called Dago Red
four bits a gallon   you bringa you owna crock
It was our only breakthru   Funeral & shrill as crows
each morning over their tubs between the backyard ledges
Maria's blackskirt sisters cawed a secret language
while they swabbed & slapped & tore & patched the shirts
of all us dirty atheist *inglesi* who imagined
they could seduce their clean Catholic daughters
God knows we tried

Rejected, fucked only academically   selfunbelieving writers
whose aging mothers back home needed cash & careers from us
wernt we downcast as well as uptight   bewitched & buggered?
Is that how you recall us   my old/young fellow-batch?
I doubt it   We cast our balances from different figures
but the column stands   elysian on the Hill
If not   no matter   since nothing does but when it's there
& beatitude alive's too fast for savoring   it's drunk like water
Yet I would stake what's left of mine
our seesaw joy still spins   whatever length of telescope you try

Italians no   but maybe we could pass for artists
poets at least   We changed at evening to scarves
climbed the crazy staircase-streets to Merto's
the only allnight blindpig on Telegraph
& sipped the one beer we could afford
ignored by Billies banged or bearded & never seeing Merto
(turned out she was in Folsom on a legging rap)
Weekday mornings of course the world beheld us
falling headlong to the Embarcadero trams
Slim in his suit   for pickles   haymow hair slicked down
me spectacled & sweatered for the Berkeley ferry
(the already greying Bay   the stillblue sky)
dangling yet more bundles of Basic Undergrad
margins bloodstained with my aborted lyrics

Ah but every helterskelter weekday we ended
crabwise on our Roman hideout   where proud as prentice guides
we clung somehow to our only City's only Matterhorn
Pharisees who knew not those on SF's other hills
hills trapped with streets   that blundered slapbang
over the cones of resurrected Francis
squealing with rollercoaster autos & trailing rails
for cable cars stuffed with their compromising tourists
On Telegraph we had no streets   what's more no telegraph
no English   no rich   no cobbles   no cement
Humanists we moved in a sweet haze of deprivation
across the windstink on our blustering seacliff
No wheels at all   not even bikes   only cavemen
falling down a ladder jungle

& overhanding up again by wood lianas
to fire & sleep in doubly-blind stone alleys
It was what we'd grown souls for
this union with the last Hopi on a cliff
a Wop Cliff at that   long floated out from Genoa
& grounded like a wobbly hinge beside the Golden Gate
Come to think of it we never missed the Bridges
the Gate's own Self was there the way Drake saw it
the Bay open   to the Philippines
& latenight ferries served as well for us
as for the suicides we never thought of joining
– no boast in that   except of luck
Maverick fleas   too wild & fond of others' blood
(like those forever in our spavined beds)
to bite ourselves   we were busy riding the backs
of all our wooden centipedes jackknifing us plumb down
to separate jails at morning's 8   & up again to Life
at sundown   whatever Life is   when capitalized
Something that whirls at least   however senseless
The moment transient as smoke   yet tall in dreams
as when a great tree or steeple catches fire

It wasn't we did a thing worth memorandum
failed to build Twat's Tower   or found the City Lights
If all were still alive on that Hill today
not one could recollect us   well Merto maybe
Merto the Great who came back at last
a gullvoiced gaunt Elizabeth the First   Virgin Hill Queen
hip & trippy 30 years too soon
She fell for Slim & bid us to her welcome-home ridotto
We'd made it   Billies of the Hill now & till death do us

A week more & our shack was empty
I had a job in Salt Lake   Susie to join me in the fall
Slim meanwhile moving to her boardinghouse in Berkeley
We'd had a mere 3 months   a something   but no Eden
I think we refused to notice that we'd left it
As if needing some last symbolic gesture of betrayal
we held our final blowout   SusieSlim&I at the snooty Mark
on the last bloodmoney from my UC galleymasters

Or did we?   am I maundering now   of other girls timespaces
It's possible   Imagination makes numerals or Venus
from the seafoam   art's not the only way to simplify the past
senility will do   or plain laziness
I tell it so far as memory's concerned
& memory's now the only one concerned
a destructive child   breaking up *tabulae* for toys
There's some things we forget to keep in mind
& others we are mindful to forget
In the end we never bear to face the truth that nothing's done
that matters   unless it flies into the butterfly
the caterpillar planned   & even that's a thing of one-day matter

The biggest stars they say lack density
but some of them spin brightest in the lens
I'd call that Hill a crazy set we wandered into
& mimed our way along the scenic edge
juggling apprehensions & misapprehensions
playing kids   fools   vintage Beats   false
citizens   real lovers
in a comical-historical-pastoral goatplay called Cloudcuckooland
while all the showplace shot toward Centaurus

At least we had no time to invent our parts
try hero roles we could be still regretting
No doubt that growing old is feeling grateful
for the disasters chosen   not even visible
as scars now   except perhaps to others
Cockaignes recalled help me keep going
skindivers rise to dive again
Somewhere in my brain pan   that Hill stands
& turns me on   we wind again our long legs with the hollyhocks
the funstairs the housestilts the geraniums   & hold on
thinking we help to keep the crooked chimneys up
Perhaps we did   until a broker's generation came to topple them
It could be we brought Arcadia just the extra weight
that stopped the whole ramshack kaboodle from collapsing
in a cloud of sawdust goatshit grapeskins

Or say St. Francis   on his last American cliff
suspended gravity & time   while mortal & imperilled
we leaned *sans souci* down to love our falling likeness
in that still blue upside sky   & then we fell

Or did we?   & which way up?
A somersault perhaps   for I'd almost forgotten
it was Slim who stayed   who married Susie
I should ask you both   how you recall it
Was it like that at all?   or cant you hear me
& this is all a letter to the dead?   you don't remember?
No matter   whatever was   our ferris wheel went round
with gusto   its motion made a tune   a living one
allegro   not death's   his rigadoon wont sound
till all that turning stops   & we are neither sideways   .
up nor blissful down   but free   for all   or nothing

1930/1970

      there are delicacies

there are delicacies in you
    like the hearts of watches
there are wheels that turn
    on the tips of rubies
& tiny intricate locks

i need your help
    to contrive keys
there is so little time
    even for the finest
        of watches

campus theatre steps

Cars lengthen up and away   like dark ferrets

THE MIRACLE WORKER   no that was last week

TONIGHT'S FEATURE is   (*PHOOOOOT!* Phooooot

diesel wheels roll   beyond the town

to Denver, Frisco,   somewhere)

Face like a pressed flower   no sound from her

as the wheelchair   is pried up the steps

the international hit   STOP THE WORLD

Night birds are chirring   over the cedars

Tomorrow at 8:30 : : :   *the Griffins are*

COMING

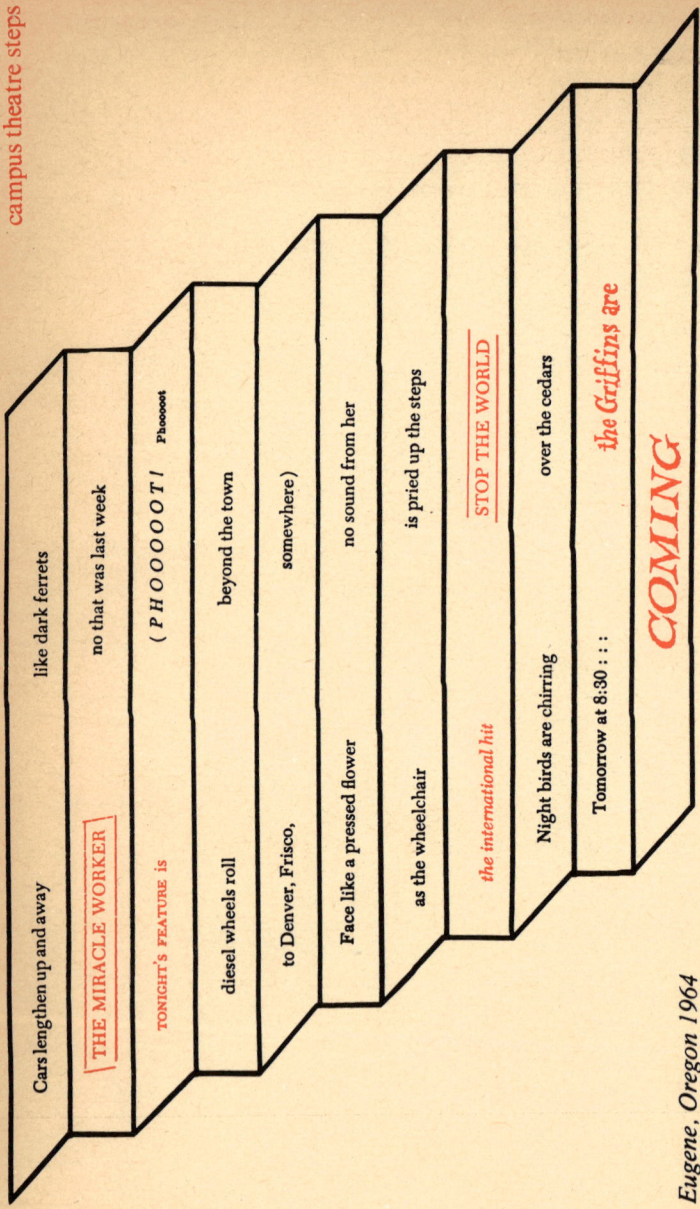

Eugene, Oregon 1964

ka passage alaska passage ALASKA PASSAGE alaska passage alas

our ship seems reefed
and only the land comes swimming past alaska pass

the
  first through   green   cresc   to the
      tramp downwards the fog in n   enDO   e   fORE/
                                                           R
                                                           E/

SHore'S pIeD coMmotion of bristled R O C K S

and blanching   d r i f
                                    t

up from a spew sp & B a   Logchute ws
      of   linters R K A A   r r o

(one mark of the few that men have scribbled on this
lucky palimpsest of ranges)

at times a shake-built shack exchanges
passive stares with Come & Gone
or eyeless waits with stoven side
to slide its bones in a
                              green tide

age alaska passage alaska passage alaska passage alaska pass

Alberni Canal 1934/1960

1

u ar e
q   s

s   f
      o
n   r
i
      s
e   t
d   e
a   e
m   p
      l
e   i
r   n

buildings a   g   buildings *are made in curves for peopling*

2

HOLD UP CEILINGS

some ***WALLS*** are said to
when perhaps they only

HOLD DOWN FLOORS

S   o
O   r
M   b
E   l
                         a
R   n
V E   d
                        l
    a   y
E   *v i*   h
A   i
L   *e*   d
W   e
A   *w*   i
L   l   s   t
L   o   l   but
S   g   l
         wa
         ha
       o   n
     l   d
  d   s

3

i like a waiting room to f l o w

let people   go   o r   ᵂan-deᵣ   sl o
                                      w
a room to   out w i t   the weather's ᶠfᶠi tttₛ

make its own   O)ᴹ(O ns & ˢʰiₙ i   O O
                                      n g N N
                                           S

a room in Public Duty being (private) beauty

4

OUTDOOR ZOO

br EATH ing   s ᴾ a Cᵉ   S
                y
            f a
         o   c
       r   h
       a n d t s
                         g r   a   s s e s

                      U
                   ᴾ   B
                    I C
               a   L   for
                   B A S I S
t   a
h p   n p
e e   d e
   n   n
n i u g c lasses   n i u g f aces
where the   ᴸ ᴮ ᴵ ᶜᵁ Pa ss   ess s s
                                           ssss
              B   ss   s   s

Vancouver 1963/70

Stanley Park, with its convenient
thruway, aquarium, totem poles
(exact replicas of originals now
stored for preservation) . . . a thou-
sand acres of playground where In-
dians once

Turning from the great islands
drowning in the morning's waves from Asia
my car heads me from the city's April
cherry petals on the slick streets
against the flayed mountains the billboards
promising orgasms of power   Tahiti   death insurance

. . . Blessed with relaxing airs, Can-
ada's Pacific metropolis, and third
largest city, offers . . .

Over the taut bridge   through the lonely park
my wheels will themselves to the shrieking
Around the highrisers the sullen leisured
dogs and the rolling realtors   Then the spastic traffic
of buyers and bought   pedlars of weed and soap
of acid and snow   of work and wonder   in Skidrow's lanes

yacht basins, beaches, golf . . . pan-
oramic view where a modest cairn
commemorates . . . British Navy in
1792 took possession of the North
Pacific coast . . . From Vancouver
the east-bound tourist may travel
the awesome Trans-Canada Hiway
thru a thou-

Eastward an hour and the master I own
has rushed me to winter and wildness
and merely the gray road coiling and diminishing
upward like a dragon's tail swinges me off
from the unsupportable Real

the tortured peaks   only a breath more broken
the blind dive of the canyons   a scratch of a century deeper
since those first compulsive whites   the Searchers
for gold   absolution   furs   or mere difference
came hurtling in improbable canoes   heavy with liquor
and fear   bearing their beads and syphilis
muzzleloaders and god
but from the truths that compel me
up this land's one nerve like a virus
to undo in a single day my father's lifetime of westering
from my own lusts and neckties and novels
from ulcers   vitamins   bulletins   *accidia*
i lie unshielded under each night's motel roof

under the uncontrollable cliffs and the starlight
falling on the same ice-bitten ranges the first men saw
in that century the Siberians took   or more
(and took a hundred centuries ago)

to move by floes and hunger past the point of no return
trailing the great woolly ones
watching for the gleam of nine-foot tusks
tracking   floundering in the newborn earth
wolving by the black rivers that rattled from the glare
of the narrowing icewalls   till the last red fountains
(*Mammuthus parelephas columbi*   his blood)
gushed on the boggy tundra at the blind corridor's end

In the nearby museum, mounted
specimens of the wild life, and a
spacious diorama outlining the
story of man. (No charge).

Surviving westward then over howling summits
to possess these still fresh-hewn alps
(which I inheriting do not possess)
moving by day through bear and elk and by their killing
outliving sleep by capturing the deer's Wit
the Power of cougar   in nets of dance and word
the medicine of mask   the threat of drum

Three mornings now from the applefoam and the seas
my Engine unreels me out from the last gouged hills
like a bull straightens into the prairie's arena
charges in a dazzle of snow the human mesh

Through Calgary, where the Black-
foot Trail once crossed, a four-lane
artery helps speed the traffic of
Canada's greatest car-per-capita
city . . . In Bowness Park, life-
sized models of dinosaurs that once
roamed the area can . . .

where all began for me   though the log cabin
where first I was forced into air is a lost ghost
under a vanished bridge by a dying river

In 1912 Stampede Day was inaugu-
rated to perpetuate the finest tradi-

An ash of ice whines at the crosses of streets
A morning drunk is spattering curses
over a halfbreed girl in a blotched doorway

Eastward again I am pulled to a sky
of land flattened white to the Pole and
drawn against the unstillable winds
the breath of that madcap virgin mother of ice
who embraced it all a wink ago in the world's eye
till the sun woke us again with his roving glance
and sent her shrinking and weeping frozen lakes
over the upstart grass

Hoarding her cold passion she lies   the Greenland lodger
and the land's long face   no more than mine   can forget
is graved with her monstrous rutting
Her time is our secret clock   She waits for all to slow
Then to lust back   wider than Europe and Pacific deep
bringing her love   the rounded silence
a long hard peace.

1965

Under the fume   of the first dragons
those spellbinders who guard   goldhoards under barrows
whole fields of warriors   wilted even Beowulf
fell in balebreath   from firedrake fangs

Yet this hugest of Worms   though he outburst heaving
from deepest of meres   under farthest den
is led leaping and leaping   at last to our shores
and hour by hour   overhewn and whelmed

Not without fury resists   flames in the night
blasts the world air   wans all blue day
Ho! a handful of thanes   in helmets threaten him
in silver keeps stab him   the old swartshiner
with gauges bedevil   with dials with cyclonesnuffers
endless they slaughter   that slimiest of Nadders

Hwaet! he is quick again   that thousand-toothed Queller
whirls his ghosts in our wheels   unleashes or locks them
Yea he lives again   in our new graveloot
breath of that sly snake   stifles and clings
slides from our long ships   coils round our steadings
Eala! we are lost   in the spell of his loopings.

Port Moody, B.C., 1964

first flight

Before i was 5 i knew
i was different   a bird   at least
if only left alone in the right place
ide fly
the polegate to the corral wd do
was out of kitchenwindow sight
    my mother
    cd watch me later   from th ground

i said a Gentle Jesus
more to warn him i was coming up
than fear i wdnt
& took off
arms flapping from th highest bar

th trouble was   i realized
just before i started howling
    somebody had been watching all along
    th hogs

later ive made my takeoffs
strictly without blabs
    to Those Above

but damned if ever ive got set
on th top rail of any gate
without i hear a rooster crow
    & sense a row of snouts
    between the pigpen slats

on the night jet

small waffle-irons glowing

on a huge farmhouse stove

crossroad towns of saskatchewan

six miles below

faint rods of highways

electroscopic genes

mainly only the stars

of farms

lonely as the others

like reflections above

and as remote from me

now

Dust blowing round the Emperor of India
George V by the Grace of God & the CPR
Cafe empty except for a waitress
who wont answer an honest hello
& cant serve beer
Back on Portage Avenue   the week's filth
attacks whirling from the gutter
Other old loners
one with a nose like a rotting peach
is arguing passionately with himself
On the corner a drunk lowers his white pow
to belch at a pair of women in levis:
　　Fi bucks fer one a *your* dirty twats!
　　woodn give yuh a fart furrit
　　yuh fuckin nitchies!
Wind blows but the stink hangs
along this deadtreetrunk of the city
In a photographers' window globefaced matrons
are shining over their oldworld embroidery
& there is a dim blowup : Portage Ave. 1901
(the same facades looking young
& the street a river of space without autos)

On the gritted pane I'm startled to see
behind me somewhere the faraway Sun
driving a last shaft between deepblue rainclouds

I walk alone in the wind and the dusk
toward the beautiful antediluvian sky

1959

unknown territory

VIRTUe

peace is our only

wolves

NADA

slam ishing
n
y
n
x

mhush
hush b

TC bogs

reel

snl

co wind S

Posterior
S

Northern Limits of

Civil Lies

CpRAN

o
p

superior

Superior joint

Inter

wage development
wes
me
n
t
system
Asian
an &

HER

gold

Canada

hostile territory

Hur o m
ock

pollution

Uncontrolal

UP

Tontonia

Taxem in coccc

Ex for

Trapshooting

missilesss

up her can nada

7.59 a.m.
despite the white flak descending
outside my window
on the black ruins of barricades
the tires are whining over
& the iced entrenchments in the ravines
i know the revolution is flowering
somewhere
or how could they be hauling captives
in paris this moment to the markets
battalions of defiant *muguet*
sold in the streets   & yesterday
the radio reported vancouver infiltrated
even here in toronto some day the rebels

let us keep pistils taut
powder dry
buds will explode   scent will be used
see the young coming   to save the world

8 a.m. . . . & now the news . . . American bombers . . .
in montreal an explosion . . . police in Belfast . . .
toronto's air pollution index this morning
 . . . i'd forgotten
it's only a vegetable revolution once again

better grab wheels & roll them south
this could be the last   it seems

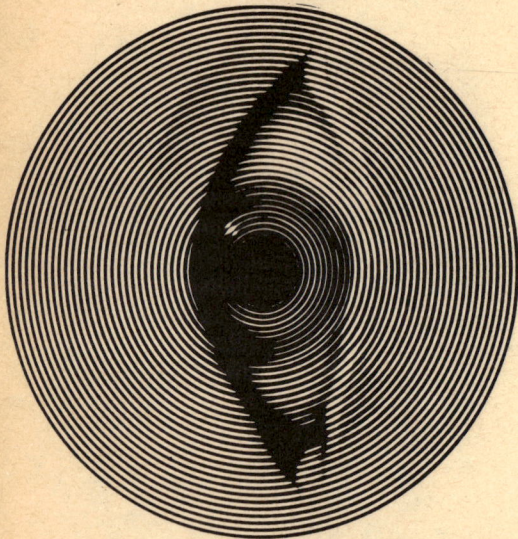

canada council

after the calorestimated 3rd meal
in the male hall they walk back
to the compulibratories
keeping to the asphalt paths
as conceived by the landtects

sometimes a thousand are in motion
engimechs the most   at 0826 hrs
in pairs   with crewcuts   hands by sides
& slightly crooked below rainbreakers (yellow)
with *U of W* on back   ENGINEERS on upper
L sleeve   & black number upper R

since none of this is actually required
nor the gloves (black)   hushpuppies (grey)
nor absence of headcovers & expressions
what is felt is campustalt   a communiternity

almost as striking   communalove   at least
the mathamen   cruts not quite so short
& sometimes grouped in 3s
in all else waterloobed
hands by sides & slightly . . . (yellow)
MATHS on . . . black . . . grey . . . absence

a few artsies still (though they're already '70)
dressed the same of course
yet sometimes carry briefcases
wear their ARTS upon their sleeves
& walk alone

1967

in purdy's ameliasburg
(for the first time, 1965)

But Al   this round pond   man –
     where's Roblin Lake   I mean the real one?
     where's that great omphalos I know
     corpsegrey below apocalyptic skies?
    this cosy girl's-belly-button
    brims with rosewater
    from one of those frilly May sunsets

Dont get me wrong   I'm grateful to be here
    after Toronto   still hairy from a long winter
    after Trenton   that raped that hustled town
it's good here it's peace the blackbirds
are setting off their own spring in the air
    but the air's too bright
it could be I've come the wrong time
    too soon for those horsecrap-fattened peonies
    you reddened the shores with
    too late for skulldeep snow
    stubborn in the fence zags
man there's only dandelions barring the way
    to that old privy

But no what's wrong is place as well
it's anybody's church across the lake
    the spire shrank
    and that carpenter who fixed it once
    against the sky is off in Trenton
    banging thumbnails and wallboard
    is you in fact
and you're not here   your mouse is hiding
quote representative of an equally powerful race unquote
and that heron   the cosmic crying rays. . .
    where in Roblin are they?

In this Ameliasburg a backyard of stones
is where they trucked off Roblin Mill
    declared historical enough
    for reassembly in Toronto
by god theyll whisk your own shack away
if you dont stop writing
    (and Eurithe too   that ferocious wife)
    (*and* the very cowpads   before your eyes)

Al I think they have   I think Somebody's
    cleaned up after your picknicking glaciers
they've raised the roof on the shack
ringed it with summer homes   told Ptolemy to leave town
made your spouse a young and patient paragon again
    It's the Same People of course
    who took the wolves away from Malcolm Lowry's woods
    repaired Eliot's London Bridge
    smoothed Jeffers' headlands back to hills
so though it's fine here   well it's not Ameliasburg

But wait   what's popping up when I sweep the kitchen?
    half an envelope   with half a poem scribbled
and from behind the battered woodheater
    yet another empty bottle   smelling absolutely
        of wild grape
Next morning I drift down a nebulous way
    to the village hardware   like a madman's museum
        Can-opener?   yep got one   got one alright
        you in a hurry?   yeah   guess it got mislaid
        I'd have to look   drop in nex week mebbe

I return under the ancient clouds
    the Lake is hazy   endless   What bird flaps away?
    the shack's doorknob turns planetary in my hand–
        Al that's your mouse   on the floor   bowing!

(a tender tale from early ca-nada)

Once there were 3 little Indian girls
Champlain adopted them from the Montagnais
to show King Louis & the Cardinal it was possible
to make Christian Ladies out of savages
He baptized them Foi (11) Espérance (12) et Charité (15)
then put them in a fort to learn their French

Little Foi wriggled away & split for the woods
but Espérance & Charité quickly mastered irregular verbs
& sewing   developed bosoms   went on to embroidery
When Champlain saw they had acquired piety & table manners
he dressed them in style & sailed downstream to Tadoussac
en route to the French Court with Espérance et Charité

But a wicked merchant named Nicholas Marsolet of Tadoussac
got Espérance aside & told her she was what he had to have
She said she had a date in France with King & God
Nick snarled he could have her & her sister given back
to the Indians   & grabbed her round her corset
She pulled a knife & got away to Charité

Les deux étudiantes then wrote Nicholas a letter
Hope began it:
      "Monsieur Marsolet, it was an honor & a pleasure to
      meet you, & I look forward to our next rencontre.
      In anticipation I have sharpened my knife so that
      I may on that occasion give myself the added joy
      of cutting out your heart"
& Charity added:
      "It will give me, monsieur, great pleasure
      to help my sister eat it."
All this sounded more elegant in the original of course
because that was in correct seventeenth-century French

They showed their letter to Champlain
He was impressed   no mistakes in tenses
He told them he was proud they had stood firm
especially against that méchant marchand Marsolet
who ate meat both Fridays & Saturdays   an Anglophile
& sold hooch to their cousin Indians in Tadoussac
However   Champlain added   he didnt think
that Espérance et Charité were ready yet for France

The two young ladies wept   unrolled their broderie
Champlain agreed they were bien civiliseés
They went down on their knees   showed him their petticoats
Champlain was kind   admired the sewing   but was firm
It was France   he said   that wasnt ready yet for them
He gave them each a wooden rosary
& sent them back to Québec with Guillaume Couillard

Couillard was a respectable churchwarden & crop inspector
no merchant   he couldnt read & had 10 children of his own
He was the first to use the plough in Canada

but when Champlain got back from France nobody knew
where Hope & Charity had got to
or if they ever found Faith again

fourteen hundred and ninety seven
giovanni sailed from the coast of devon

52 days   discovered cape breton n.s.
caught some cod   went home
with 10 bear hides
(none prime)

told henry 7
his majesty now owned
cipango   land of jewels
abounding moreover in silks
& brasilwode
also the spice islands of asia
& the country of the grand khan

henry gave giovanni 30 quid
to go back to nova scotia

who was kidding who?

halifax

"periodically sleeps between wars" (Hugh MacLennan)

Today you can see his dozing bones
under the mange of his fur
poke him and he scarcely stirs
curled in the big den
the glaciers rooted out for him
Rum secretly fuming in his old brain
belly with a memory of molasses and fish
he is coiled in dreams of Covenanters
and clowndances to the redcoats of Cornwallis

Foghorns never wake him nor bells of buoys
nor the sly tides that pluck his toes
not even the steel wool of the seawind
rubbing away at his haunches

It takes each generation's crack
of doom and then he stumbles out
young again and getting educated
chucking his sailor's cap
rolling the girls on the park grass
running a new jack up the citadel
totting up the lost convoys

Bear Halifax
surly in your matted pelt
bear that once tore your own entrails
with a great wound — and licked it whole
and ugly as ever –
bear with your paws at the end of rails
and your ass a port shitting for the world's wars
    sleep well
    the next one will wake you dead

1945

```
N E W f o u n d l A N D
n e w f O u n d L a n D
n e w F O u n d L a n D
n e w f O u N d l a n d
n e W f o u n d l A N d
n e W f Ó u n d L a n D

N E w f o u n D l a n d
n e w F O U N D l a n d
n E w f o u n d L A N d
n e w f o u n d l A N D
N e w f O U N d l a n d
n e w F o U N d l A N D
n e W f O u N d l A N d
n E w f o u N d L A N D
n E w f o u n d l a N D
```

pei

O here is an isle
where the sands run for miles
but the lobster's not here for the plucking
the water's berg cold
the ladies not bold
& only Milt Acorn says fucking

them able leave her ever

1. can. lit.
   since we had always sky about
   when we had eagles   they flew out
   leaving no shadow bigger than wren's
   to trouble even our broodiest hens
       too busy bridging loneliness
       to be alone
       we hacked in railway ties
       what Emily etched in bone
   we French&English never lost
   our civil war
   endure it still
   a bloody civil bore
       no wounded sirened off
       no Whitman wanted
       it's only by our lack of ghosts
       we're haunted

2. our forefathers literary
   had little laugh or quippery
   even Can. Lit. profs are still uncertain
   of Haliburton
   & all their students reassembling
   Carman's skeleton
   never found the funny bone
   (beware the jokes of Archibald Lampman
   they'll give you cramp, man)
   Grove was grave & Mair still more
   & though they made a Baron out of Gilbert Parker
   his prose just went on getting darker
   Sir Charles G. D. Roberts couldn't see
   in all his g.d. woods   Silenus in a tree
   – well yes there was our northern loon our Leacock
   subtle as a duck   & laughing like a peacock

Like an eddy

about turn

ROCK

flying

turn around

swallows but

1965

i think you are a whole city

& yesterday when i first touched
you i started moving
thru one of your suburbs
where all the gardens are fresh
with faces of you
.flowering up

some girls are only houses
maybe a strip
development
woman you are miles
of boulevards with supple trees
unpruned & full of winding
honesties

so give me time   i want
i want to know
all your squares & cloverleafs
im steering now by a constellation
winking over this nights rim
from some great beachside of you
with highrisers & a spotlit
beaux arts

i can hear your beat-
ing center   will i
will i make it
are there maps of you
i keep circling   imagining
parks fountains   your stores

back in my single bed i wander
your stranger   dreaming
i am your citizen

if only someone else would come
(from endre ady's hungarian)

To show how i loved
i rushed you the wild
  hungry
     troops of my desires
the proud Hordes of the blood

i envy
  pity
    detest you
my lucky slut
    my regal moocher
    of tail

if only i could want someone else
  as i want you
o if she would come
  a different woman   another
    anybody

hokkai in the dew line snow

to sleep under real
stars   wake in the pupil of
original Sun

goodmornings with birds
love naked by waterfalls
o best planet –   whoooM!

a north door opens
the leaves scurry to hole and
the Cat prowls our world

1.

ESPECTACULAR
ESPLENDIDA
ESPONTANEA
ESPORADICA
ESPARCIDA
ESSENTIAL
ESTRELLA
ESSER
ESPOSA
ESPUELA
ESPUMOSA
ESPERANDA
ESTUPENDA
ESTRUENDOSA
ESTIMULANTE
ESTRAMBOTICA

2.

o what can i do for my little grey mare
& what must she do with me?

im hardly a horse at all anymore
a wrinkled old bonebag is all
& she, shes a colt & kicks her small legs
over the fences & into new grass

when im in the corral & ass to wind
she bites me out walleyed & morose
to run in the sun with the fillies
& whinnies ahead like a yearling

o how can i keep with my nipping old mare
& how can she wait for me?

if you were here

that bowl of greenery on my table
would look as if it should be there
the salal leaves would shine a glossier olive
& i would say its berries
are pumpkins growing for the chickadees
& you would smile & finches in the spruce would sing
if you were here

we'd walk up the toteroad to the bluffs
past silent flames of sunstruck leaf
where hummingbirds are zooming in for sweetness
& we would glimpse a doe with a bird-fragile faun
& maybe hear an eagle shrilling from the cliff
along that trail where no one goes
since you're not here

around the shack the broompods crackle in the sun
but no one listens no one stops to finger
the silver sheathes the wild pinks wear
or touch the papery bracts of everlastings
or the blue bloom
that lights the globes of oregon grape
but you would touch

as from some soundless warp of time i watch
but not with you – the great ships of oceans
come swirling thru the sparkling pass below
while over them at dusk the baldheads glide
the tallest firtops sway in secret dance
& – see! – sunset's firing ice along the Olympics!
but you're not here to see

galiano is. july 1970

the marriage

now we've agreed
to be each other's house
any tent will do us

we'll pitch on this beach
dig the butterclams
make alderhooks for seaperch
eat the berries by the spring

in time we'll find a way perhaps
to use this driftwood
to keep the tides
from ebbing every day

still

like eddies my words turn
about your bright rock
rock bright your about turn
words my eddies
like words my eddies bright
turn about your rock
rocklike my turn
about your bright eddies
your bright turn eddies
like my rock about you

still

1971   PNOME   1971

JANISSARY

```
            1  2
 3  4  5  6  7  8  9
10 11 12 13 14 15 16
17 18 19 20 21 22 23
24 25 26 27 28 29 30
31
```

eloi   ogg

CASSIWARY

```
 1  2  3  4  5  6
 7  8  9 10 11 12 13
14 15 16 17 18 19 20
21 22 23 24 25 26 27
28
```

mai chin chu

MARSH

```
 1  2  3  4  5  6
 7  8  9 10 11 12 13
14 15 16 17 18 19 20
21 22 23 24 25 26 27
28 29 30 31
```

abe rillway

RAPERY

```
       1  2  3
 4  5  6  7  8  9 10
11 12 13 14 15 16 17
18 19 20 21 22 23 24
25 26 27 28 29 30
```

jan s waring

MAJOR

```
                1
 2  3  4  5  6  7  8
 9 10 11 12 13 14 15
16 17 18 19 20 21 22
23 24 25 26 27 28 29
30 31
```

fred v waring

JUBILEE

```
    1  2  3  4  5
 6  7  8  9 10 11 12
13 14 15 16 17 18 19
20 21 22 23 24 25 26
27 28 29 30
```

marcia prill

AUGUSTIN

```
          1  2  3
 4  5  6  7  8  9 10
11 12 13 14 15 16 17
18 19 20 21 22 23 24
25 26 27 28 29 30 31
```

d c m burr

TIMBER

```
 1  2  3  4  5  6  7
 8  9 10 11 12 13 14
15 16 17 18 19 20 21
22 23 24 25 26 27 28
29 30 31
```

toby gnome

HOG TOE

```
          1  2  3  4
 5  6  7  8  9 10 11
12 13 14 15 16 17 18
19 20 21 22 23 24 25
26 27 28 29 30
```

bernault femmebeurre

BURN OFF

```
                1  2
 3  4  5  6  7  8  9
10 11 12 13 14 15 16
17 18 19 20 21 22 23
24 25 26 27 28 29 30
31
```

m burgeon

EMBER DAY

```
    1  2  3  4  5  6
 7  8  9 10 11 12 13
14 15 16 17 18 19 20
21 22 23 24 25 26 27
28 29 30
```

jeanne ouaire

SOMBRE

```
          1  2  3  4
 5  6  7  8  9 10 11
12 13 14 15 16 17 18
19 20 21 22 23 24 25
26 27 28 29 30 31
```

ossip m birrock

Pnomes are gnomic mnemonic pomes to remember things like the
kooks of the monk and who wrode them.

poet-tree 1

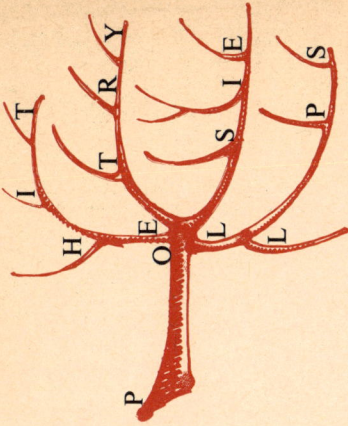

poet-tree 2

i fear that i shall never make
a poem slippier than a snake
or oozing with as fine a juice
as runs in girls or even spruce
no i wont make not now nor later
pnomes as luverlee as pertaters
trees is made by fauns or satyrs
but only taters make pertaters
& trees is grown by sun from sod
& so are the sods who need a god
but poettrees lack any clue
they just need me   & maybe you

"there is an insistent tremble
from the night's drinking"
    not that
      but this
      not *a*
        but *the*
        way
          to read
with the night's tremble
the way
    to make
      the poem
        the scene
        the baby
everything gentle
    even wistful
especially the lock
    of hair
      that claws
        for attention
and must be sadly
    trembly
      beautifully
      pushed
      away

Vancouver 1962

for maister geffrey

In Chauceres haselwood wher Robeyn pleyde
Wher wren remembreth that the phenix seyde
Wher Janus breeth blowth myrrh on misteltine
I walken wol til al hys joy beth myne.

Her from hys montaigne den a grymme leoun
Bombleth benigyn, the queynte scorpioun
And every fiery serpent venymous
Hath wyn of pitee in hire een; the mous
With deyntee toon stalketh in bourde the boor
(The tusked swyn that wayteth evermoor
In pryde the bord of Noel to begynne).
Her glyden grisly tigren without synne
And oliphauntes blowen trompes of joly soun.
I fare in feeldes of meditacioun
By boles blake and coy camelopard.
Ther sely ounce byteth on the swarde
Hys owne tayle, and al is sikernesse.
Ther coursen croppen without tikelnesse
(O brighte horsly hors of Lumbardye!)
And dredeles the hertes with hornes hye.

In Chauceres haselwood I walke alweye
And never thynke out of hise shawes to streye.

London 1959

jukollage no. 1

)————————————(

this is my song
        petula clark
i got a feeling
until you love someone
every little bit hurts

  hey darling
i can't get enough of it
i'm a man
        englebert humperdinck
going down for the third time

the river is wide
i will not cry
till it's time for you to go
sad story

)————————————(

childrens prayer to santa

Santa send me soldier clothes,
Ray guns, rockets plenty,
Santa send me all this now
Instead of when I'm twenty.

3	little	words
any	day	now
	what	can
the	matter	be
no	milk	today
drowning	my	tears
tiny	bubbles	release
me	i'm	alive
i	wanna	be
	aware	
in	the	ghetto
long	time	blues

```
U N I V E R S I T Y
U N I V E R S E D
U N V E R S E D
U N S E R V E
U N E V E R
U N I T E
U N E W
U N O
U N
U
```

All Stephen Leacock Associates
are most cordially invited
to the celebration of the Leacock Centennial
to be held at Trent University. . .
It will be a town and gown evening,
beginning with a corn and weiner roast
on the banks of the Otonabee
and will flow onto
and about
the podium
outside of
the new Bata Library,
for which the architect Ron Thom
has won several international
citations.
The rest of the open-air evening
will be marred
by readings,
turn-of the century songs,
minglings,
skits
and odd
happenings.
No lectures;
no speeches.
–God
save the Queen.

Mariposa, Orillia, News Packet, Spring 1970

while i'm drinking a cup of coffee
(free translation from óscar óliva)

while i'm drinking a cup of coffee
i start revising the poems ive written

what a mess   so many lost words
why did i carve into my chest
& claw around in my miseries?
to look for what?   a sea
neither clean nor habitable

if ive written *loneliness   tree   mud*
it's just word-fuzz   it means i'm stretching
my arms   and overturning the clock
(showing its nakedness & pathways)

once i was hung up on obligations
wanted to give men nothing less
than lightning

but now i'm sleeping under an image
ive doubled it over   to underline it

tomorrow i'll wake up in a new world

Irvine, Calif.1968

window seat

40 ft of wing out there
suddenly i want to walk
into that sun
but capt loudspeaker says
headwinds 105 mph speed another 400
at once im walking back on air

!BUT WHAT A FUN DEATH!
                                    alt 35000
                          nothing but
              7
         miles of
high dive
at last i can practice   k   n
      g   c   i
    a   a   f
       i   j   e
r s   n   s
      e

                        o   a   r
                    b   d
s   p   r   i   n   g   i
                                         n
d o w n   g
       from   c l o u d
                        to   c l o u d

(o yes acceleration 32 ft per sec per sec).

but ive 7 m to play with
& all that wind d r i f t
& b o d yf l a p

ive got time at last to break the world
's record for b (i once dreamed about) s o m
              a   e
                                             r
              c   s
              k   a u l t
                                             s
before straightening into
              AA
              SS
              WW
       N N AA N N N
         N N NN N
              Ɐ

so widearmed & precise i am

embracing s e e !
             e e

the whole world & time
in one last sweet tick of li--

but no one lets me walk out
too hard to break this doubleglass
i'll have to be content again
with the usual smooth landing
dead on
& the meek shuffle into the pens
to wait my turn somewhere
at ground level
under the overcast ahead.

Edmonton 1969

I was busy extending my patchwork of lint & batten
from ankle-sores down to my new heel & toe cuts
absorbed in masochism & blessing my foresight
to carry bandaids   blessing too the first voyagers
who brought breadfruit trees to Fiji   & thanking most
the man who planted this one to cast a benison of leaves
just where the bare volcano trail widens to the islet's road
– though (i'd conceded to myself) there were some million years
of hindsight before the breadfruit learned
it must grow 3-foot leaves & cannonball-sized seeds
to come to terms with perpetuity. The cottonbatten foliage
on my purpling feet however   argued i'd learned
nothing much myself   at least from 60 years of print
about coral poison   or the agility of lava
in slicing through Canadian shoes

I was cossetting a raw big toe with my last band
when i grew conscious there was a soft slow pad of other feet
approaching down the trail   so close when i looked up
i was caught in the pitchy stare of eyes deep-locked
in a great ochre face   *Bula* i said   trying to get it bass
& guttural   His huge eyebrows rose like wings
Bula bula! he said quickly & stepped back a pace
I must have got my hello close   & thought that now
he'd give the broad Melanesian grin of welcome
But his eyes were black ivory & the long bones of his face
seemed set in suspicion   even hostility
I could read nothing   nor guess his age
the face rough leather   but the blast of his hair
burst up sootblack as any youthful native's
He was my height & about twice my width   standing silent
like some ageless tree of flesh on the sharp basalt stones

Suddenly he spoke   but in Fijian   I fumbled out my 7 words
to say i couldnt speak his language after all
He went back to staring   & i self-conscious to my toepatch
Rooster-crows had been filtering thru the mangroves
There must be a village close   & he from it
I tried to forget it was near here only 90 years ago
these natives ate their last missionary   A bulbul
began bulbuling in the breadfruit overhead   then stopped
No sound but the far surf breathing   & us 2

Mis-e-ter   *yalo vinaka*   he groped as painfully for English
please wat name-a you?   Erola i said   *what's yours?*
He spoke something cave-deep & gruff   no way i could repeat it
I was about to try standing & shaking hands when his arms
flew wide & made a gesture at the road
you wait-a for a (he made a toot-toot) *bussy?*
His tone perhaps was only puzzled   His eyes
shifted from my feet to the broken shoes beside them
I told him yes i'd been swimming in the old crater falls
was trying to get back to the guestlodge in Port Levuka
He dug some of that i think   but threw out a massive chest
made swimstrokes with his arms   & waved towards the lagoon
Wy you no−?   *Swim in the sea?* i filled in   & tried
against a steady wrinkling of sepia forehead to tell him
i'd been skindiving all week till i got rolled on coral
& the Levuka doctor told me to stay off reefs
till the sores healed   & then today i'd cut my feet on scoria
– but i'd lost him near my start   Brows like furrowed walnuts
he bent over me   mouth-muscles agonizing to find
the right sounds   *Year* he said *how mucha year you?*
Sixty-five i said & fingered it   For the first time he smiled
Me! he said nodding his tall pompom   *me too sickyfi'*   *Io!*

It was worth all the struggle to see that spark
leaping our wordgulf   We were egged on   I learned
he'd even heard of Canada   *far side Hawaii*
& that he'd been born in the village beyond the trees
My lord   i thought   he's only one generation
from Cannibal King Thakembau   I began pulling on my sox
& asked him if he'd been to Suva   He shook his black busby

Sa sega   *No alla tima here*   He looked more proud
than sad   With a square mahogany finger then he made a circle

You?   you go round worl'?   *Yes* I said *Io*   & felt ashamed
He turned as if satisfied   but swung back & flung out
the question he'd wanted to ask me from the start
Er-ola wat wrong you FEET?!   I tried again & got nowhere

This wasnt tourist country   he'd never met a fullgrown man
who went all the way to the volcano & never looked for boar
who swam in cold waterfalls   & in the sea without a spear
who wasnt even hunting conchshells
But most of all he couldnt understand what hurt my feet
And so he stood   a black-red statue of Melanic Power
round storm of hair   maroon cheeks & torso cicatriced
with the darker scars of tribal rites a half-century old
his only covering a chamba skirt of sorrel colored reeds
& all mounted on two pedestals of ancient meat
two huge flat sun-barbecued tough plank-steaks of feet
like those his cousins use   across the bay on Benga
to walk on white-hot stones   for magic or for tourists

What wrong my feet   i said   *is I not born here too*
He laughed   the only time   with a wide flash of solid teeth
Bussy come sometime   he said gently   *you be o-right*
Ni sa mole Goobye   He went paddling swiftly down the road
You o-right now   i called   & lay back to wait the bus.

Ovalau 1969/Galiano 1970

Knotheaded men in seaboots all the way from Hokkaido
crowded on a moored fishtank built like a tug
They've been catching tuna   for rice   & sharks
for the fun & fins   drying on the rigging now
along with tails & swords of swordfish
Down the scale-slippery wharf comes a five-foot Dr. Moto
in impeccable shorts   with a size 1 ½ wife behind
Tipsytoe they are the new nobility of Fiji
Chief Cannery & his Lady come to greet the Sea Chief
Tunaboat Captain Sato   & bear him to their hill villa
for ceremonial rum & saki with the Paramount Chiefs
the Aussie Prince of Port & the New Zealand Ratu of Fishmeal
The Captain Chief will sing them his voyage: a full catch
unloaded at Pango but much spoiled & sold for catfood
The present cargo in fine condition but nearly lost
by confiscation when they were found inside the Tonga limits
But they'd cut their lines in time & said they'd come for cocos
Tuna getting scarcer   too much Korean competition . . .

The sweaty sailors meantime are heaving great fish
one by one from hold to deck to wharf to truck
Some are hoping there'll be time before sailing back
to find a Yankee beer   & even a halfcaste school girl
at the one whorehouse up the one street

The British are all back in Suva plotting to set Fiji free
The Indians are keeping the shops
& procreating

There are no Fijians in view

kiwis

Up there in Canada we might say weirdo　　　or screwball
Down under here it's weird bird　　　pronounced weed bed
Strange phrase for a put-down　　　considering the emblem
of New Zealand : a wingless tailless chicken
feathered shagreen & shaggy　　　& breathing through the far-end
of a 6-inch macaroni tube　　　Still　　　the oddest birds
are human any place　　　& hunted by other humans
the Even Ones (in New Zild: the Vest Mejerrty)

That night I was to give a public reading on Z campus
Its English Department in the afternoon received me
standing for sweet sherry　　　& sitting down to bitter tea
Three departmental poets kindly autographed their books
(I'd brought)　　　& then they left　　　regretting
they wouldnt hear me since they were reading their own poems
at the same hour in another building

I was meditating how to outploy that exit
when the Head asked me in dulcet Oxcam to explain
what rally does go on in those creetive-writing-shops-
ay-think-you-call-them I told him what went on in mine
then Miss MacSomeone　　　a small termagant
whose 5 wheelbroken Chaucer students I'd already met
explained that New Zild students were fay too serious
to fend tem for thet　　　we've British stendids you see
though Ay could quite believe thet in Amirrica. . . I left

Out in the dim hall a bearded youth beset me
Please just *look* at them　　　he jabbed a scribbler at my chest
& flipped pages　　　his eyes still probing mine defiantly
Masses of pencilled verse　　　but sketches too　　　His gaze
was almost evil　　　For a moment I was back on the dark stairs
of the Clichy Metro buying a feelthy packet that later
proved to be postcards of statues in the Louvre
But lord these were no fakes　　　good audiovisuals
shapomes in Swiss and Brazilian contemporary modes
Tim was just old enough I could take him off for a beer

It seems he had a girl in London who sent him Little Mags
He planned to join her but was still in debt to shrinks
after a breakdown when he was flunked out from the U
flunked by one of the 3 tame canaries in the English Dept.
They ole think Oim bonkers   he whispered over the bar table
(as if we were really Underground)   But he thought I'd dig him
I dug   then asked him why the local bards had cut me out
Ah he said   it's cause the Ead asked D to be yer Cheermin
Cripes! I said   he's my friend   & your best-known poet!
Thet's ovaseas   here they think *they're* tops Tim said
& D's been divorced & publishes settires in the dylies
He eynt square enough for them   Ha! I said I see
D's a weird bird!   Roit said Tim   a weed bed loike me
loike you too   Check! I said   & we had another beer

Next day at the zoo I saw my first live kiwi
A young keeper brought it tucked underneath his arm
like Anne Boleyn's head   It wasnt much more animate
He placed it on the announced area of grass & time
the zoo's P.A. had been promising the sky all day
It promptly whacked its long nosebill in the turf
& froze   hunchbacked   splaylegged   shuteyed
while the keeper (quietly in love with the creature)
explained it was a nightbird   shy under flashbulbs
(there were I'd say about 30 cameras clicking)

I think myself with his long schnozzle that kiwi
was quietly turning on to audiovisual worms
wriggling stubborn underneath New Zealand's Weed Bed soil.

christchurch, n.z.

I have just flown 1100 miles from Australia
& landed in a Victorian bedroom
They sent up cindered muttonchops for lunch
There is an elderly reporter in my room with pince-nez
He wants to know why I have sideburns
& if I dont think being patronized by the Canada Council
isnt dangerous for my art or dont I feel I need to suffer?
In stone outside my window Capt. Scott
is nobly freezing to death near the South Pole
Suddenly I know the reporter is right
Sideburns have been sapping my strength

tongareva atoll

Some women's combs are turtleback
glowing like brown moths
in the dusk of their hair
but the heads of the younger chicks
shine with duraluminum stars
their boyfriends / the pearldivers
hammer out from Yankee bomberskin
(a Liberator crew in '45
thought the torches of night fishers
was their airstrip)

The population here is 685
not counting tortoise & oysters

There may be enough plane-carapace
to last until the next Liberator –
or so the divers & the turtles hope

The oysters as usual say nothing

They're waiting for the night
the great pearl in the skyshell falls

strine authors meet

No tram   taxi dumps me on wrong side of the unknown
I climb through a maze of academic alleys   5 minutes late
blunder into a middleclass quagmire lapping up sherry

A female macaw beckons me   the local Edith Sitwell?
     Yew the kin eyejin gander gisses a lecher?
     Jus gonna read pomes
Her bill falls with alarm
     Yer nat gander read peartree? Ow long yer gan an fer?
     I allus go on till the chairman stawps me.
     Aow   (she takes my arm firmly)   yid better talk to im

We walk to the table head past place cards for 60   Cripes!
     Ow yea-yes Misser Binney   ow surrey   Misser *Ben*ny
     We been waytin fer yew
I can see the sherry's gone
An ancient fat man he sighs   but affably i think
     Rid semmena yers once about a kin eyejin fren jew add
     was killed at Deeper summers
Before I can figure that out & say thanks he's warning me
     this the Fickle Tree Club   we got to be houtbee tin
     and pipple still kemmenin   wont get stetted til Apis hate
     and henyule meeting kems festive curse
     be lucky tev affenahr fer wotayver yew intindin tew dew

We sit   The muscular arms of the lady on my right
have found a worthy opponent in the chicken
I interrupt her battle to express genuine pleasure
to see so many of the city's authors here tonight
But this one's a realist   modest too   between bites
     Affefems jis spouses   uzbints   woives   or frinze
     loike me   oim only the voice prisidents woif
I ask about the macaw down the table
     ow *err* she roits fiction   nuvvles   foive so far
She told me their names & the macaw's   nothing rang a bell

I'd slipped on my homework   Who was her publisher?
                                        continued:

Ow aint nennem peblished   but she's read em all to us

Nine already & still eating   Not being warned
my show was private i'd asked my young friend M
for the reading   By now he must be wandering the campus too
I told the chairman   who hadnt heard of M or of his book
(last year's winner of the national first-novel prize)
          Allem seats is pied in idvence   an allem sowld
          (He smiled) Sivn dollars a plight   Yer ena trek shun
The buggers i thought   they got me free   not even tramfare
and begrudge a chickenbone for penniless M
I tell the chairman i'm leaving to find M   He shrugs
          Iffey dan moind settin anna floor
I tell him M can have my place   I'll read standing
but just then M comes in deadpan with two young poets
They squat in the darkest back corner

The business drones on to 9.30   when the chairman introduces
a gentleman with a white goatee & stammer   who introduces
Mr. Buh-Beaney   & sits down at 9.45
The chairman huskily reminds me i've only 15 minutes
I decide to dedicate them entirely to the far corner

First a hands-across-the-commonwealth   let's make it
Frank Scott's *The Canadian Authors Meet*: "Expansive puppets. . ."
& now a glimpse of Canada's romantic north : Purdy's piece
about the dangers of shitting among huskies   followed by
a small statement of my own poetics : "how fucking awful
it is to be a poet" & finally a Bill Bissett "hare krishna"
chanted   walking out with the only three writers in the room

museum of man

The trustful curator has left me alone
in the closed wing of the aboriginal section
What's here? 3000 spears from Arnhemland waiting
for a computer to calculate their principle of balance
– but what's in those wooden drawers?   i peek
sheeezz!   shrunken heads   from new guinea
& dozens upon dozens of twelve-inch penis sheaths
I'm going to lock doors   plant spears at windows
& try on everything for size.

loggia dell' orcagna

heisting in his left hand
the longsnakehaired head of medusa
perseus with his right
shoves out his well-endow-ed sword
     over the drooping boston hippies
     sitting soretoed on the stone benches

nearby lions
their manes in curlpapers
jiggle small white worlds
precariously in their paws
by steps where florentine children hop
     & 2 brown japanese are turning
     with dispassion
     their color cameras

1963

song for sunsets

goodnite sun
im turning over again
im on the little ball
so slowly rolling
backwards from you

i hope youre there
central & responsible
burning away
all thru the black
of my dumb somersault

i'll tumble around
& wake to you
the one who never sleeps
never notices
too busy keeping the whole
flock of us
rolling towards vega
without losing
our milky way

goodnite big dad
hasta la vista
hasta luego
we'll switch on now
our own small stars
lie in darkness burning
turning
through unspace untime
& upsadaisy back
i trust to you

HAREKRISHNAKRISHNAHAREHAREHAREKRISHNA

H
H H H H
H H
H H

A
A A
A A A A A
A A
A A A A

O
O O
O -m- O
O O
O

R R R R
R R
R R R R R
R R R
R R R
R R
R R
R R

E E E E E
E
E
E E E E
E
E
E
E E E E E

KRISHNAHAREHAREHAREKRISHNAHAREKRISHNA

acknowledgments

to jack mcclelland, my publisher, for continuing to be

to bp nichol, & his generation, for turning me on, & to bp
especially for his aid in developing certain visual ideas
in this book, & giving several of these poems first public-
ation in *grOnk*(series 4), toronto, ganglia press, 1969,
under the title *pnomes, jukollages & other stunzas*

to juditte sarkany, for providing the literal translation
of the endre ady poem on which i have improvised here

to the following periodicals, in which some of the poems
in this book originally appeared:

england:
ica bulletin, mainly, priapus, tribune,
verse & voice

u.s.a.:
alaska review, best poems of 1968,
cimarron, hanging loose, new, northwest
review, potpourri, quartet, southern poetry,
sparrow, university of utah pen

commonwealth:
arena (n.z.), *meanjin* (melbourne),
poetry australia, poetry singapore

canada:
b.c. historical quarterly, black moss,
blew ointment, canadian forum, delta,
elfinplot, imperial oil review, merry
devil of edmonton, nue vue, other
voices, prism international, quarry,
queens quarterly, saturday night,
skylark, tamarack review, u.b.c.
chronicle, west coast review